With Best Wishes

With Best Wishes

Barry Bailey

ABINGDON PRESS
Nashville

Library of Congress Cataloging in Publication Data

BAILEY, BARRY, 1926-
  With best wishes.
  1. Sermons, American. 2. Methodist Church—Sermons. I. Title.
  BX8333.B24W57   248.4'876   81-20632   AACR2

ISBN 0-687-45842-0

Many Scripture references herein are the author's paraphrases.

All Illustrations Are by
Gerald S. Moody
Book Designer

Cover photo by Earl Cox III

MANUFACTURED BY THE PARTHENON PRESS AT
NASHVILLE, TENNESSEE, UNITED STATES OF AMERICA

This book is dedicated to
my wife, Joan, and
our children, Barry and Janice,
and to my mother, Marguerite Bailey

Acknowledgments

This is the third book that Abingdon has published for me, and it has been a joy to work with the editors. I am also deeply indebted to Gail Cooke, who edits my sermons each week, and to my secretary, Eugenia Hinds, who types my sermons and directs the mailing every two weeks. They have helped me greatly in publishing this book.

Preface

For years now I have frequently concluded my letters with the phrase, "With best wishes." Many of us often say, or hear someone say to us, "Have a good day." These phrases may have a great deal of meaning, but there are times when they can become empty clichés. If I tell you to have a good day at a time in your life when you are going through a heartache and I am unaware of it, you will recognize immediately that I am not dealing with you as a person. When I write letters, I do not always know the circumstances of the people who will receive them. It seems to me that in order for our language to have the most meaning, it needs to be related to what is taking place in our lives. For this reason, I have entitled this book *With Best Wishes,* and have tried to deal substantively with problems we live with periodically. Only when we know where each of us is and have some idea of what we are feeling, can we tell someone, "Have a nice day," or send them greetings "With best wishes," and mean it.

Contents

With Best Wishes

Waiting

Waiting is sometimes torture. We can wait for a letter that never comes, a phone call we never get, a promotion that is never offered. We long for things that we feel we have a right to because we see other people receiving them. But they may not come to us. We long for love, for someone we can love personally who will love us, for someone we can trust and feel close to who trusts us. But we may not find such a person. So we wait. All of us have had such periods of waiting. At times, just when we think we have what we have been expecting, it's gone. We reach for it and, like a sunbeam, it's not there. Every one of us, at one time or another, has known what it is to wait.

"O Lord, how long?" is the biblical cry repeatedly heard in the Old Testament. There is probably never a period, now, or in the history of humanity, when that lament is not heard. It was heard in the Israelites' captivity in Egypt. While they were in the wilderness, they wondered when they would be delivered. Then they went into "the land of milk and honey," and for centuries were longing for the Messiah. Later, during the Exile, they thought that perhaps they would never go back to their homeland. When they did return, they began to ask the question even more. In Palestine, under the heavy boot of their enemies, controlled by first one country then another, year after year, they kept saying, "O Lord, how long?"

And then, although his birth was not as they thought it would be, Jesus was born. Many Christians say that the Jews "missed" him because they wanted a Messiah. I say that the Christians also missed him, because we want him to be a Messiah—although we call him a Savior. We want him to be a Messiah because we want God to do our work for us. We think, "God, come on a cloud to solve all of our problems for us. God, give us world peace. See that enough money is given for all the causes in the world so people can live together." We can be so smug and talk such a marvelous game. We want God, in His mercy and love, to do what we never want to do ourselves. We, too, say, "O Lord, how long?" And wait.

People in agony around the world can relate to this cry—those who have had their homes and lives devastated by earthquakes, floods and fires. People who wait in hospitals, afraid, sometimes penniless and lonely, can relate to this cry. Those who have so much going for them, but still feel empty, are also familiar with this lament. It seems we never really have it all together, do we? Older people in geriatric homes wait, children in children's homes wait. Even members of what we think of as conventional families know, at times, what it is to wait.

There are times when the help we waited for can be dangerous. Some years ago, the State of Louisiana put on a campaign called "Drive Friendly." The idea was to drive carefully. I suppose if you had a wreck, it was to be a congenial collision! One woman was carried away with this campaign. Seeing a car stalled by the side of the street, she stopped to ask the driver if she could help him. The man accepted her offer and said, "You will have to get me up to twenty miles an hour because I have automatic transmission." "All right!" she replied, and got back in her car. You can guess what happened next—he looked in his rearview mirror, and there she was—barrelling down on him at twenty miles an hour.

When you sit and wait for someone to help you, and you look in a rearview mirror and suddenly realize what kind of help you are going to get—that's frightening! There is a time when waiting is agonizing, even dangerous, but we have to go through it.

At other times, waiting can be hurtful, almost destructive. I knew a kind and gentle man who felt very deeply but was not articulate. He didn't handle words artistically. Sometimes I think a lack of fluency is deceptive. If a person can express himself with ease, others may assume that he feels deeply because he expresses himself so well. That is not necessarily so. It's not that the fluent person is putting on an act, but he may simply convey more than he really feels, and we may hear more than he intends. It is possible for someone to feel very deeply and yet, for whatever reason, to be embarrassed and awkward about putting his feelings into words. That is the way this man was. He loved so much, but was only able to convey the merest suggestion of his feelings. It was extremely difficult for him to say things. The more profoundly important something was in his life, the less able he was to express it.

His business prospered. He made a great deal of progress, and after years of work, he planned a special celebration. This occasion was going to be one of the happiest days of his life. The party invitations were printed, ready to be mailed, and then there was a family argument. It wasn't a mild disagreement, but the devastating kind of quarrel that can happen in a family when people say harsher things, perhaps, than they intended. The family was practically torn apart and someone decided that they could not have the party.

The other family members really didn't talk to the man who had planned the celebration, nor did he express himself very much; that would have been out of character for him. He had lived too long being verbally passive. If you are sensitive, you know what his feelings were when the party was cancelled after he had waited for it so long. Days later, the man and his wife took the party invitations out and burned them. The celebration never took place.

Waiting can be agonizing, even devastating. Sometimes we wait for things even while knowing perfectly well that they will never come.

Waiting, however, can be our hope. There is a time when waiting is one of the most important things we can do. What's worse than rushing something, making it develop before it's ready? We wait for an idea to explode. Jesus did that in his preaching. Timing for him was extremely important. "How many things I want to tell you," he said to the disciples, "but you are not prepared to hear them yet." In any great drama the climax of a play must come at the right time, when the audience is prepared to be involved so that they can hear and understand it. There is a time when we wait because we hope.

In the story of Lazarus, recorded in John 11, Jesus was away in another town, and word came to him that Lazarus was dying in Bethany. Jesus said to a disciple that Lazarus' illness was not unto death. If that statement was true, then Jesus did not raise Lazarus from the dead because he simply had not died. If he did raise Lazarus from the dead, then Jesus was mistaken in saying that he had not died. Obviously, this material must be read on several different levels.

If you say "I believe in the Bible," that doesn't mean just reading and believing the words. You don't even know how to read the Bible unless you think about and interpret it. Biblical study is not just reading the words. You could teach a parrot to recite words! You must understand them, too.

According to the story, Jesus waited two days before he went back to Bethany. How does that sound to you? If you sent word to a friend that you needed him in a hurry, and he waited for two days before he came, you would be disgusted. However, the fact that Jesus waited two days is critical. When he did arrive, Jesus asked, "Where is he buried?" and was taken to the grave. He was told that Lazarus had been in the grave for four days.

From some people's point of view, the human mind of Jesus is supposed to know everything. Some present Jesus as a know-it-all. If he knew everything, why didn't he know where Lazarus was buried? He was the truth, but living in a body, just as we are, and with the same kinds of human limitations we have. That is why his love is so profound. If we claim he was omniscient while on earth, that robs him of his quality, the cutting edge of life. I think he would say the same sort of thing about himself that I am trying to say about him.

When they came to the grave, Jesus asked some people to roll away the stone. When they had done so, Jesus said, "Lazarus, come forth!" They took off the graveclothes that had been wrapped around the body, and Lazarus was alive. Perhaps Jesus might have been able to raise Lazarus from the dead—make the corpse come back to life. That might have been what took place. But that's not a miracle that would make me want to follow Jesus. Every so often you read an account of someone being pronounced dead but coming back to life. If this happens in a hospital, you don't begin to call the doctor "God," and start a new religion. We are long on being religious—short on truth, but long on religion. To be dead and then be alive is not a miracle, it happens once in a while.

If you think I don't believe in a miraculous understanding of God, then I am not saying this very well. I don't believe in a miracle meaning we break God's law or God breaks his law. If that is our understanding, I think our conception of God is too narrow. God never breaks his law to get back into his world. God doesn't have to intervene because he has never left his world; God is already here.

Let us suppose that Jesus waited two days to go back to Bethany because, although Lazarus had been walking around for some time, he was not really alive. I imagine Lazarus to have been like we are so often—dead to life, dead to issues, principles, and quality. Suppose Jesus loved him, but couldn't get through to him. Jesus

wouldn't run down there the minute someone said he
was needed, if Lazarus hadn't listened to what he had
said in the past. Jesus took his time. Now, when he got
there, the time had come when he could say to Lazarus,
"Come forth, be alive!"

It takes more presence of truth in your life to awaken
you to issues than it ever would to bring your body back
to life. As a matter of fact, Lazarus later died. Some
might ask, "Jesus, why didn't you wait around and bring
him back to life again?" Or, if going to heaven was so
important, why was Jesus tampering with the process in
the first place? We can assume that Lazarus went to
heaven, unless we have the idea that only a certain kind
of nice person goes to heaven and Lazarus was just not
that respectable. The Bible does say that Jesus ate and
drank with sinners! Yet, when you read the Gospels you
also get the idea that the sinners are going to heaven
ahead of the Pharisees. If Lazarus had died, you would
assume he was in heaven—so why was Jesus bringing
him back from heaven?

There is a great truth in this story. Let us imagine that
Lazarus had been waiting to live, letting the moments go
by. He was going to *wait* his entire life. That is hell.
Think who his best friend may have been—Jesus. Even
his best friend couldn't give Lazarus what he needed. So
Jesus waited a while. Two days later, he went to Bethany
and said, "Lazarus, are you ready? Your people, the
Jews, your ancestors have waited a long time and you
have also waited a long time. Now I want you to come
forth!"

When Lazarus came out of the tomb, the onlookers
took off his graveclothes. You and I ought to try that for
ourselves—try removing our veils of prejudice, of

smallness, the views and ideas that bind and hamper us. We know how we live. We want Jesus to perform the unusual miracle of bringing a dead person back to life. But we don't want to hear the truth. It takes more presence of God through Christ to wake us up to issues than it ever does to work with our physical bodies. We wait, and by waiting, we surrender the possibility of joy.

I think Jesus could have brought Lazarus out of the grave, although that wouldn't have mattered one iota. It might have impressed us, but why would Jesus have done it? So we might believe in him? What is meant by "believing in Jesus"? It means we know that he has the truth. What was the truth he was teaching? He was teaching compassion, love, justice, mercy—but he was not trying to impress us. Do you think Einstein would have been thrilled to impress a freshman physics class? Not at all. He could have done that any day of his life, just by being there. But Einstein must have been thrilled when some student could get a glimpse of what he was trying to teach!

We are very much like Lazarus. We keep on waiting. We keep saying, "God, give us world peace," but we don't like people. We say, "God, make our families happy," but we don't want to forgive anyone. "God," we keep praying, "I want to be a Christian—but not yet." And so we wait.

Now there are some things for which we must wait—eternal things, for instance. Or on a more mundane level, we wait for a telephone call, a letter, someone to visit us. But we should never wait to live. Real living is always now, from the inside out, not from the outside in. So we must "come forth!"

In order to stop waiting and really live, we must

realize that the Messiah never comes bringing instant, magical cures. We will never find an external panacea for all our problems. We can learn that from our own experience. Maybe you had a problem in college, and so you changed schools. If that did provide the answer to your problem it was because you found the answer internally, and not just by the physical change. This principle is true in every area of our lives.

With the presidential election occurring every four years in our country, we face the recurring problem of expecting the next president and Congressmen to take office and solve our problems for us. They cannot do that. One of the difficulties an incumbent president faces is that he must run on his record. And the voters know that he couldn't solve all the problems in his first term, so his popularity tends to be at a low ebb. With someone new coming in to office, we think it is going to be different—and, to a degree, it may be. We want to say to the government: "Straighten out our national economy, but don't adjust anything that would affect our local economy." We are like that. We want to solve our problems nationally, but we don't want to be forced to adjust personally very much.

We change parties and presidents. Finally, they, too, have to face the hard decisions, and when they don't solve our problems, we want to say that we are disillusioned. The truth is that we never should have expected a panacea or a simple solution. Although we really know that answers will never come externally, we demand that it be so in government and in life. But solutions never come that way. We live from the inside out and not the other way around.

We have a tendency to drive ourselves into believing in a crisis theology. At least, if we are not careful, we live by a crisis theology in our relationships. For instance, sometimes a man doesn't let his wife know he loves her until she is about to leave him. A student doesn't study until he or she is close to failing. Some people don't start to really work until they are threatened with losing their jobs. Aren't we often like that? And some people do not take religion seriously until they are threatened with the prospect of hell. In that case, they don't care about issues, they just don't want to go to hell. And the student who waits to study doesn't care about learning, he just doesn't want to make an 'F.' A crisis-oriented behavior doesn't really involve changing, it is just adjusting a little bit to outward crises in a burst of agitation.

Throughout our country we often hear the idea preached that the world is going to come to an end soon. Many say that every sign says that Christ will soon come back again, and this preaching is received enthusiastically by some people. But this is silly. Jesus is never "coming back again," because actually the spirit of the Lord has never left us! I believe the real question is not, "Do you believe Jesus is coming back again?" but, "Do you have to be threatened with the world coming to an end before you take your life seriously?" If the only way you are going to care about honesty is by being threatened with the end of the world, then you don't care about being honest. There has to be a better reason than that.

Someone once sent me an advertisement sent out by a television preacher. It contained a picture of the building that he owns, showing Christ holding the building. The ad asked you to sign your name on the enclosed form and list your financial problems, your personal problems, or anything else that was bothering you that you wished to mention. Then your letter would be buried under the building so that it would be part of the foundation of the building. I think that is blasphemy! Do you think that would please God? I don't. That makes about as much sense as consulting a witch doctor in darkest Africa and asking him to stick pins in a doll so that you can control someone. Both of these ideas are superstition.

Christianity is becoming popular in America today. But I want to say as clearly as I know how that from my perspective, the brand of Christianity that is gaining approval is superstition, voodoo, and sickness. Others do not have to agree with me. Yet, under the name of God, they have to ask where truth is and what the truth says about what we are doing. Does popularity affect truth? What would it mean if everyone voted today to repeal the law of gravity? Nothing, it would just expose our ignorance. We do not control truth; truth judges us. What does it mean for an idea to be popular if the idea is wrong? When I hear it said that many people follow this brand of Christianity, I couldn't care less, other than that I hate to see them so wrong in their beliefs. We do, indeed, practice a crisis kind of behavior.

Suppose a woman sends some money to the man who circulated the ad to have her name put under his building. Perhaps she sends him ten dollars that she really needs. Maybe she is ill and lives alone; she can hardly write her letter because she has arthritis. If she sent her money to me at the church I serve, I would want to say to her, "You don't need to do this, God loves you. You need to keep this for yourself."

Christ didn't come to make your church great, or my church great, or anyone else's organization or institution great: he came to show us love. At its best, religion is supposed to free people so they can understand that. What does it mean for our churches to prosper if people live in hell? "How long, O Lord?"

Each one of us needs to hear the words, "come forth!" When a young man of Nazareth went to Bethany, he might, I think, have been able to raise Lazarus from the dead. But that kind of display didn't appeal to Jesus. He had already wrestled with the temptations in the wilderness and decided, "God, I'm not going to try to impress the people with some kind of trick just to show them my power. I want to show them the nature of what You are and I'm going to do it even if it costs me everything I have."

Suppose Jesus waited two days to go to Bethany because he wanted to let Lazarus decide whether or not he wanted help. Would Lazarus listen? Would he get rid of his smallness, smugness, prejudice, the idea of trying to make God his size, or whatever his problems were? Jesus would wait, and when Lazarus could hear, he would go. Two days went by. Jesus wasn't waiting to waste time, he was waiting for a purpose. The day came and Jesus asked, "Where is he?" The people took him to Lazarus and Jesus said, "Now Lazarus, are you ready? I want you to be you. I want you to be what you have never been, but could become. Lazarus, come forth!"

Jesus calls us today by our names where we are. The greatest miracle in the world is not to bring a corpse back to life. It is to take us, in our world amidst all of those things that would bind us and keep love from being real, and bring us back to life. Christ speaks to us, he calls us by name and says, "Why don't you come forth—now!" Let's not wait any longer.

2
When You Don't Get What You Want

All of us know what it is not to get what we want. We can recall many times when we have been disappointed.

We normally read the incident at the wedding feast in Cana, recorded in John 2, as a miracle story. But I would like us to think more deeply about it. We need to ask what the implications are if we read it in that way. What does it mean, if what Jesus did, with all of his mind and his ability, was to take some water and turn it into wine in order to save his host embarrassment? What does that "miracle" say to our world?

If you want to come to grips with reality, you must also take Jesus' temptations seriously as they are recorded in Matthew 4 and Luke 4. I don't think you can take both incidents seriously as they are usually read in the Bible. You are either going to make a mockery of the temptations and decide Jesus didn't mean what he said, or you are going to have to determine that the young Galilean did, indeed, make up his mind what he was going to do, that he said, in effect, "I won't cater to the crowd. I will love them, but they can't buy me. They didn't give me what I have and they can't take it away from me."

That sort of statement would indicate the manhood of the Master. Can you catch something of his spirit, his psyche? He was born in Bethlehem; Joseph and Mary had to flee with him to protect him. He returned to Nazareth, and to a great extent, he was ostracized. He went to the synagogue to preach his first sermon and was run out of town. People thought he was peculiar, strange. That certainly comes through in the Gospels, which clearly say, "People were disturbed by him."

We do not believe we would be like those people. We think we would follow Jesus and love him because, in our narcissistic state, we make him like we are. We make him small enough so that we are comfortable with him and then we say, "I believe every word of the Bible!" How can we make that claim? What about the temptations? Jesus wrestled with that dilemma and said, in effect, "O God, I'm not going to trick people or impress them. I'm not going to throw myself off a steeple and have angels save me so that people will say I'm great and then follow you because of a display." Jesus had too much integrity for that.

When people were in the presence of Jesus, sometimes they felt better, could think more clearly, and they felt that they were healed. Notice that after such a healing, Jesus always said, "Your faith did it, I didn't do it for you." Jesus knew that the people were going to become ill later and eventually die. He knew the bodily healing wasn't permanent. I think he was trying to say to them: "Don't put your confidence in the fact that you are physically better. Have you caught what I am trying to teach? 'Blessed are the meek. . . . ' Do you see what I am dealing with? Don't follow me for the wrong reasons."

Jesus was wary of popularity. This is demonstrated by the fact that when people were, at times, healed, Jesus would ask them not to tell anyone that he did it. He didn't want people coming to him for that reason, although he was interested in healing the body. If somebody sensed that he might be the Anointed One of God, the Messiah, the Savior, he would always say, "Tell no one." We must take his temptations seriously. He decided he was not going to put on a show and try to impress people.

When he was back home in Nazareth, Jesus, his disciples, and his mother, Mary, went to a wedding in the neighboring town of Cana. This is said to have been the first miracle. And there is a miracle here, the most powerful kind of miracle in the world! However, the trouble with us is that we spend all of our time at the sideshow and never go to the main tent. Jesus went to Cana of Galilee where there was a party, the wedding. The guests were having a good time and then the host ran out of wine. This was not a big deal; such a shortage can easily happen. But Mary came to Jesus and said the hosts were embarrassed because "they have no wine." Jesus asked, "What do you want me to do?" Turning to the servants, Mary said, "Do whatever he tells you."

There were some thirty-gallon jars nearby, and Jesus told the servants to fill them with water. They did as he asked. He then told the servants to take out some of the contents of the jars and give it to the steward of the feast. The steward tasted what the servants brought to him. What I am going to say now is my understanding of the

story—I am taking the temptations seriously in inter-
preting this text. Let us suppose that the water was still
water when the steward tasted it, but that he was being a
gracious gentleman and didn't want to make an issue of
the matter. There was plenty of water. The guests
caught the spirit as they drank, and said to the host,
"There is no point in your being embarrassed. Don't
spoil this day, it's too important to you and your family.
This is fine, you've saved the best till last!"

Perhaps Jesus did take the water and make it wine. If
he did that, then there are many questions we might ask,
such as, "God, why don't you feed the people in
Calcutta, the children whose bellies are bloated by
starvation? We need a miracle performed. God. You
did it once, do it again!" God has never worked like that
and that is why God doesn't work like that today. Don't
you know that? We are not likely to know God as long as
we misread the Bible.

The children are starving in Calcutta because there is
not enough food. These problems are not in the world
because God is sending them to us to punish us; the
problems are here primarily because we are selfish.
Granted, sometimes we do not know enough to solve
the problems that confront us. At times, we want to do
better than we are able to. But I think our problems are
basically caused by our selfishness.

Let us try to take Jesus' temptations seriously. If we
do, we need to ask what Jesus did when he was dealing
with the water. Could it be that he told the guests that
they had plenty of water and to drink that? Then what
would have been changed in Cana? The people. And
that's the miracle! The greatest compliment anyone can
pay you is to let you become a part of the answer. If you

go to a counselor for help, a good counselor realizes that he cannot solve all the problems for you and so he invites you to solve your problems and he assists you. If someone gives you all the answers, what does that mean? It means that you do not grow at all.

At the wedding in Cana, I believe Jesus did what is always consistent with his life. "The kingdom of God is within you," he said. The kingdom of God is like the mustard seed—it can grow, develop and flourish. We may have a problem, but we also have the potential of finding an answer. It is not water becoming wine that makes a difference, it is people changing their attitudes.

Jesus performed a miracle. It is the kind of miracle we always need, and it is the most difficult to perform. He worked with the people and they were changed. Imagine that I came to your home. You might offer me a Coke. I would say that I'd like to have one. You discover that you do not have a Coke so you offer me coffee. I say that is fine and you serve me coffee. You didn't change the Coke to coffee. Someone could repeat that incident later and assume that's what you did. The drink is incidental. The visit, the being together, is what matters. You did not change Coke to coffee, you worked with me—and that's fine, I would just as soon have coffee. In this way you see a miracle performed on a much deeper level.

Do you think there is more integrity or authenticity in water becoming something other than itself? We should not fail to appreciate anything in its natural state. Let a child be a child; why must a child be an adult? Let an old person be that, in the beauty of being older. Let each thing be as it is. There are places on our earth where having water would be a miracle; water is needed, not wine.

Unfortunately, there are times when we create our own problems. While that is not always the case, we are too often like W. C. Fields, who said that he always carried a bottle of liquor with him in case he saw a snake—which he also always carried with him! When we create our own problems, we then want someone else to come and solve them for us.

At other times, our problems are forced upon us. A lot of us face difficulties that we didn't bring about. We can feel guilty and blame ourselves when these externally imposed problems occur, but if we did not create these problems, we shouldn't labor under false guilt. We simply do not cause a lot of the difficulties in our lives that we have to face.

I once pulled into a service station where another customer was having water put in her radiator. The nozzle of the water hose fell off into the woman's radiator, and the service station attendant couldn't get it out. He worked on it, but it became evident that he wasn't going to be able to retrieve it. The woman cheered him on, telling him he could do it and urging him to keep trying. Finally, though, he convinced her that it was impossible. "What am I going to do?" she asked. "I don't want that nozzle in there!" I liked his response: "I won't charge you for the nozzle."

There are times when things just happen to us that we do not want and did not cause. Young people especially need to realize this. They can often be threatened, frustrated and ill at ease because they get the idea that a lot of people are against them. Welcome to the club!

Almost everyone else has felt the same way at that age. It's just the way we are.

However, whether our problems are created by us or forced upon us, we have to learn to face them. We cannot ever be intelligent enough to avoid them completely; we cannot be wealthy enough to be insulated against them. There is no way we can build fences around ourselves. Even if we became hermits, it seems to me that we cannot entirely avoid problems. As a matter of fact, I think the more mature we become, the more problems we are going to face, because we are more vulnerable. However we define success, the more successful we become, the more wide open we are, because there are more people who can get to us and hurt us. We just have to learn to roll with the punches. We never become "religious enough" to be protected from problems. Jesus faced more problems than we will ever face in our lives, and we will never be as good, as loving, and as caring as he was. We have to learn to have some kind of resiliency.

A family by the name of McLean lived in Virginia during the Civil War. The first two battles of the Civil War were fought on property owned by Wilmer McLean. This frustrated him so much that he decided to move because he didn't want any more battles fought on his land. He bought some property and moved quite a distance away—to a place called Appomattox! As you know, that is where the war ended. General Grant and General Lee signed the peace treaty in Wilmer McLean's new living room. The people in attendance for the signing became so excited that they started to pick up mementos; they tore curtains and virtually stripped the poor man's house. Can you imagine a war starting on your property and winding up in your living room?

That is not only a historical fact, it is also sometimes the way things go with us. We do not always get what we want. While there are many things that we cherish, many things for which we are thankful, there are also certain things that we would like to change drastically. This is true of all of us. No one is exempt from this predicament; we are all very much alike. The more successful we become, the more mature we are, the more we are involved in life, and the more vulnerable we become. What do we do?

So often, when we are confronted with difficulties, we wish that someone "out there" would solve our problems for us. For instance, we want world peace, but we don't like others in our world. So we pray for world peace and talk about world peace but, let's be honest, we don't want to alter our circumstances. We want to keep what we have, and we want those other people to be happy and leave us alone. How long will the Third World be content to live on crumbs when they know we have more? Not forever. They are as human as we are.

Even though we say, "O God, we want world peace," we really don't. We want security. We can say, "Jesus, give us a miracle! Take the water and make it wine; take our hatred and make it peace," but we don't want to adjust ourselves. We can be the same way in our families. We say we want those in our families to love each other, but there are times we don't want to apologize and ask forgiveness. We sometimes would rather wring our hands and say we don't understand why our own families can't be as happy as others are. We want an external miracle to come and make our families happy. We want someone or something out there to come and solve our problems for us. After all, we are Bible-believers, and we ought to be happy.

When confronted with problems, some of us are apt to delude ourselves. In a sense, we hypnotize ourselves into thinking that we are happier than we are. We sweep everything under the rug. We need to realize that, if our families are going to be happy, the miracle must come from inside. It's not an external change. Our problem does not stem from the outside, it comes from our own attitudes and beliefs.

A recent movie dealt largely with the efforts of a family to reach each other. The family members reached for each other but always missed. They were distraught, very much like many families in this situation. There were happy times but also periods of frustration and hurt. In one scene in the movie, the mother stood by her teenage son while the father prepared to take a picture. The mother wanted to love her son, but I guess she did not know how. The young boy wanted to reach out and love his mother, he needed to so desperately. But all his mother could do was stand there rigidly, giving the impression that she resented even being in her son's presence. Finally she snapped, "Give me the camera and let me take the picture!"

The mother didn't really care about taking the picture, she just didn't want to be that close to her son. In a moment he turned his back and sat down in a chair. Did that mother need a miracle worker to come and make her family happy on the outside? No. She needed a change in the way she looked at herself, at her son, and at her life. If that had happened, you couldn't have kept her from reaching out and putting her arm around her son.

We say we want our families to be happy; we say we want our world to have peace. "O God," we say, "give these things to us!" God wants to perform a miracle; God can perform a miracle. God, through Christ, can work with us and the Holy Spirit and perform a miracle, but it will come internally rather than externally—inside us, not in our circumstances.

Naturally, there are times when we need to change external things in our lives. We may sometimes need to change a job, a location, or a personal relationship. Someone may be ill and need an operation. There are certain external things that we need to change, but we have good minds, we can figure those things out.

The real miracle, always, occurs when we change the way we look at life, the way we see circumstances. A friend once told me about a time in his life when he was depressed because he was facing so many problems; he was barely hanging on. Most of us, if we live long enough, eventually reach a similar low point. My friend dealt with his depression by looking around for people he could help, because he found that helping somebody else also helped him. That's a great attitude!

My friend also told me that, during this period of depression, he walked into the house one day and flipped on a light switch. For some strange reason, that activated the clock-radio. The radio began to play, after not having worked for months. A song was being played, he said, with just the words he needed to hear. He thought, "This is like a miracle, I'm hearing just what I need to hear almost out of nowhere." He bought a copy of the song so that he could learn the words.

If he had heard that song at another time, it probably wouldn't have made any impression on him. It was a case of his being receptive; a change in the way he saw and heard things. We want to see beauty, yet we walk around it or by it, until one day we stop to look at a flower. We want to love people, and they are all around us. One day you look someone in the eye and realize that that person wants to love, too. We have to be in the right frame of mind. Those who can sense it can see it and celebrate the life of God; those who cannot, stand there and say, "O God, let me see a miracle performed!"

Jesus, his mother, Mary, and his disciples were at a wedding. The host ran out of wine. Someone might have said, "What are you going to do, Lord? Are you going to put on a display to impress us so that we will know how great you are?" Jesus could have said, "I've already worked that one out. I'm going to let you be a part of the answer. The water is going to stay water. How are you going to handle that?"

The guests could have said, "This is just right, don't spoil the day. This is better than the first." They celebrated and had a great time. There was a miracle at Cana. I think it was that the presence of Jesus was able to change people. And that is the miracle that each one of us needs.

3
Interruptions

We often have the idea that if only we become religious enough, our lives will be smooth and uninterrupted. Such is not the case. I suppose Mary, the mother of Jesus, was religious, yet her life was filled with interruptions. At one time she was a young unmarried woman and she was pregnant. That is certainly a threat, a disruption.

From our point of view, we can smooth this over by saying, "Mary, how fortunate you were. God chose you of all women." It is true that, for centuries, so many Jewish women prayed that they might be the one to give birth to the Messiah. They did this hoping that God would act, that their baby would be born as the Messiah and lead their people. They expected all kinds of things to happen after the birth of the Messiah. But a baby was born to Mary. This brought her joy and happiness probably beyond our ability to describe, and it also brought her pain and heartache beyond our ability to understand.

However, we are less than realistic if we do not see that Mary's situation threatened her; her life was interrupted. She did not need a baby; she was not married. She was no more comfortable with her condition than any one of us would be; she was unmarried, having a child, and telling people that God did it. The people would not believe her story then, and we would not believe it today.

There is another, less popular, biblical story that suggests that Joseph is the father of Jesus. Joseph and Mary were together and went to Bethlehem for the baby to be born because Joseph was of the house and lineage of David. Think of riding a donkey from Nazareth to Bethlehem, a trip that took several days. That would be uncomfortable for anyone, but imagine how it was for this couple, as far along as Mary was in her pregnancy. When they arrived in Bethlehem, there was no room for them; the only place to stay was the stable where the baby was born. There is not much comfort in either version. Whichever way you want to look at it, Mary's life was interrupted.

Joseph and Mary were frightened and they had no money. One of the reasons we know they had little money is that they offered two pigeons when Jesus was dedicated at the temple. This was nearly the smallest offering they could make. It is tantamount to offering two pennies. Isn't it interesting that Joseph and Mary made an offering of two pennies to the God who had everything, when dedicating, of all people, the one whom you and I speak of as Lord and Savior, the Savior who could love more in a fleeting moment than the rest of us ever could during all of our lives?

Later, when word reached Joseph and Mary that

Herod was going to kill every male child two years old and younger, they fled to Egypt. Wouldn't you say that also interrupted their lives? Time went by, and they returned to Nazareth to live. Yet all the time the cross was just a few years away. We can say, "Mary, you are so fortunate to be the mother of Jesus." She was, and I suppose she would say without any hesitation that certainly she was. But if we simply see the surface, the sunshine, the joy, the laughter, the sound of the angel's voice, we misread the whole story.

Life is hard on many of us. At times, it is easy for us to feel sorry for ourselves. But one of the problems in feeling sorry for ourselves is that it cuts us off from other people. Perhaps we do have a serious problem: maybe it deserves our attention for twenty-four hours a day—for a while. That is understandable. If we are going through a crisis, we should go ahead and give the problem all the attention we can and deal with reality. So periodically, we may find ourselves with our hands full, unable to help anyone else. But it is often regrettably true that those of us who are not facing any kind of crisis often spend our time so concerned about our own hangnails that we deafen ourselves to the cries of those who are really suffering. Life is hellish for a lot of people.

I know a man who ministers in the downtown area of Fort Worth. He does a marvelous job of working with people who are the "have-nots"; people who are, in a sense, on the outside. While these people obviously need financial help, they also need spiritual and psychological help; they need a friend, and he is there.

I once asked him to tell me something about what he had done lately. He told me about a mother with two children, whose total income is $187.00 per month.

Naturally, she was depressed. I like what the man said to her. "I want to tell you something," he said. "Did you ever realize how much ability you have?" She grinned and said that she didn't think she had much ability at all. "But," he persisted, "you are finding a way to live and exist on $187.00 a month. I don't know many people who have that ability. You are surviving, you are coping, and you are keeping your family together. I think that takes a great deal of ability."

He was right, although maybe that is not the kind of achievement for which we would want to be congratulated. But it is true that life is hellish for a lot of people. We see this in South America where one dictator after another takes over. We read in the newspaper that hundreds of people have been killed, sometimes thousands slaughtered. Perhaps it would drive us crazy if we actually saw this happening because we can't do anything about it. Yet that is the kind of world we live in, the kind of world where life is painful for so many people.

Our lives are continually being interrupted. Sometimes the interruptions are devastating, and sometimes we can chuckle about them. I was at a luncheon not too long ago with several other people from our church. We were seated at a round table, thoroughly enjoying being together. Just as we were about to leave, I knocked over a full cup of coffee. It spilled all over the woman I was sitting by, almost drenching her suit. There was no way I could blame the accident on anybody else. I just felt ridiculous. I apologized and grabbed a napkin in an effort to help as best I could.

The woman was so gracious. She said, "Barry, don't worry about it; the coffee is the very same color as my suit!" You can't beat that for a response, can you? It's a blessing if someone can be color-coordinated when you make a mistake like that. I know she didn't enjoy that accident and I certainly didn't, but there are times when things like that happen.

I recently lost my overcoat. To be truthful, the coat was too expensive; I should never have spent that much money on a coat in the first place. I wish I could say that in some religious moment I gave the coat to someone who needed it, but that is not what happened. I simply lost the coat, and it made me sick. My wife was out of town when it happened, and while she was away, she had bought me a hat to go with the coat. I'm glad to have the hat, it will look nice with the gloves and scarf I have to match the coat. That's the way life works once in a while, and when it's an interruption such as this, you might as well laugh about it.

Quite often, there are interruptions to families. The two main occasions when a family will have problems are at a funeral and at a wedding. The difficulty at a funeral is understandable—someone has died and we hurt. In addition, there are so many other emotions that come to bear at this time. Sometimes we feel guilty about disagreements or broken relationships. We have not always been thoughtful and kind. Perhaps we felt more than we were able to convey, and now we feel guilty because we didn't express ourselves. Family problems occur at a wedding perhaps because of the numerous details needing attention. Perhaps the wedding dress didn't arrive on time. So many things can go wrong and often many of them do. If there is ever a time in our lives when we are going to feel threatened, it is at a funeral or a wedding—and some people feel that these two events are almost the same!

We feel interrupted when such events come into our lives and then we feel guilty because we cannot deal with them. We don't feel that we can go to someone and say that we are physically and emotionally exhausted, that the way our family is falling apart is getting to us. There are all kinds of issues that we feel we can't deal with because there's so much smoke that we cannot see the problem.

Holidays can also be interruptions for us. Christmas and Thanksgiving are times when family members are supposed to enjoy each other; we are supposed to have a good time. But we bring our personalities with us into these celebrations, don't we? We don't suddenly change at a holiday—nor should we, because no one would recognize us. We may act a little nicer, or be a little kinder, and that's great, but we are ourselves. So, sometimes we feel a certain kind of threat during holidays.

We may feel that other families are happier than ours. We are not jealous to the extent that we would want to trade, we just wish we could find their secret. What we don't know is, if those other families are real, they are probably just about like we are. They sometimes disagree and have misunderstandings; they sometimes feel threatened. Then they reach out, touch each other and are back together. All of us do all kinds of things in an effort to try to find each other in life.

Sometimes a holiday is a threat to a family because it emphasizes the idea that we *ought* to be happy, love each other, and be close, and we suddenly realize that we are not. It is not that special occasions are so hard on us, they simply bring to our minds things we feel we should possess that we seem not to have; there's a void.

It would be helpful if we could look at past interruptions from the present security. When we read the story of the birth of Jesus, we can view Herod's decree and the flight into Egypt from the standpoint of Jesus being Lord and Savior. There is a marvelous statement in the Bible that reads, "All things work together for good to them that love God." That does not mean that everything that happens is good. It means that you are more likely to bring good things out of bad things when your heart is right. When your heart is right, you can work things towards good even though they are bad.

Therefore, when you remember a sad experience of the past, look at that experience from the security of your present; get yourself in the best frame of mind and then see that experience in the larger context. Suppose someone badly mistreated you five years ago. Perhaps you would be foolish to trust that person again—I am not proposing that you completely overlook such treatment. You are supposed to use your mind to think. But even though perhaps you should not trust that person again, you should not be dominated by the fact that someone hurt you five years ago. That experience is gone. You should now be able to view it with your mind, your psyche, from your present security. You have grown and developed. You are not the person you were. So you can see that unhappy event, that interruption, from a larger perspective. This is the way we are to see life.

If we do not change our point of view, then we can see all of life through the fact that somebody hurt us five years ago. If all we can know is that Herod issued a decree and was going to kill every male child two years old and younger, we never know the Savior. Regrettably, that is the way we so often live. We get hurt and we stop. We remember what people have done to us; we remember past wars; we remember that people don't like each other and probably never will. We pick up on the interruptions of the past, impose them on the present and, by doing so, block out our lives and never see a star. We need to reverse that thinking, although not in a sentimental way. We should remember the past, we know what Herod did; but we should see past interruptions from the standpoint of a present security—view them from a larger perspective.

A friend of mine is an authority on baseball. I once asked him if he remembered a player by the name of Lon Warneke, a man whom I knew many years ago when I was growing up. "Yes," my friend said, "I knew him well." Lon Warneke was a pitcher for the St. Louis Cardinals and, as it turned out, my friend was once on a team playing against the Cardinals. The game was a strategic one going into the playoffs towards the World Series. In the last of the ninth inning, the Cardinals were on the field, the player in the batter's box had three balls and two strikes, there were two outs and the Cardinals were ahead 3-2.

It was then, said my friend, that a very unusual thing happened. The Cardinals stopped the game and sent in a relief pitcher—it was Lon Warneke. While he was warming up, he threw seven pitches, seven fast balls, almost like greased lightning right across the plate. Then the game began again, and the next pitch Lon Warneke threw was a curve ball that struck the batter out. The

game was over because the batter expected a fast ball.
After seeing seven fast balls, anybody would think that
the eighth ball would be one, too.

We live the same way, expecting the present to be like
the past. Sometimes that is wise, and sometimes it is
devastating. If all we can see is the fact that Herod killed
the children, we never get an idea of love being alive in
our world. If all we hear is the love, and we forget the
reality of the destruction, we become sentimental. You
know what has taken place in your life. If someone has
hurt you, recognize it, but you should also see the past
from the standpoint of the present—in a larger
perspective.

Frequently people profess Christianity in order to find
a solution to their problems. Because their lives have
been interrupted, they turn to the Bible or the church,
seeking a panacea. Although we try to pretend
differently, Jesus did not accomplish everything in his
birth. He is our Savior, but what difference did that
make to the world thirty minutes after he had been
born? Or, in all reality, what difference did it make five
or six years after he had been born? Jesus was just
growing up with his family in Nazareth.

I'm not trying to be cynical, simply realistic. What do
you think was going on in America when Jesus was born
in Bethlehem? People were living in America and they
did not know about his birth when it occurred, nor
would they know about it for centuries. How were they
introduced to the gospel? Christians said, "We must
convert those Indians, they're heathens!" But look at
the trail of tears we led them down and the pain and
agony we caused under the guise of being missionaries
and converting them. The unbelievable destruction that

we brought into the lives of the Indians is inexcusable. But we had the gospel, and we were going to convert them. About all that meant to us at the time was to put clothes on them so they wouldn't embarrass us, teach them the English language, and keep them sober so that they wouldn't fight.

How long did it take the gospel to come to America or, for that matter, how long does it take the gospel to reach anywhere? At the time of Jesus' birth, it wasn't known in Mexico or South America. Jesus was born, that was all. He was the truth and is the truth; he was the Savior and is the Savior. However, just the fact of his birth did not make that much difference in the world. What does make a difference is our taking his birth seriously, because we are in this, too.

God does not force everything to work out. God did not give us a baby as a panacea to save the whole world. We are supposed to be loving persons ourselves; we are supposed to be kind; we are supposed to be Christ-figures. That which was in Christ is supposed to be in us. Jesus' birth did matter, but not in the sense that it was one act which would suddenly revolutionize the world without our involvement. We are supposed to be transformed and become loving people ourselves.

I don't think that we can ever hear the voice of the angel until we go through the interruptions. Mary's life was all but torn asunder, but she kept these things and pondered them in her heart. The day would come when she could reflect and know why she had heard the voice of an angel—because she was a loving person. I don't think we can ever hear the marvelous redemption of life until we can walk through the pain and the interruptions of life.

Many years ago in Warsaw, Poland, I was entertained, along with several other preachers from America, by several Polish families. They had prepared a cake to serve us for which they had sacrificed and saved ingredients for weeks. The cake was something they did not make for themselves. We could hear the voices of children running around, and we realized that we were going to be served and the children would not be. Someone proposed that the children be brought in so we could all join together, and the cake was cut so that everyone could at least have a taste.

That was in 1959. Things were difficult in Warsaw then, and they are threatening and difficult in Warsaw today. There, on the second floor of a downtown building, we ate a cake that some loving people had prepared for us after carefully saving those ingredients. Do you know what I think we had in Warsaw that night? We may have had Holy Communion, called dessert. When you take the best you have and share it with friends or people you love, what do you have?

As it was for those people in Warsaw, life is also painful for a lot of us. Your life may have been interrupted, but you have waited. You have continued to grope and sometimes you have walked in the dark. Perhaps you are still working at it; keep it up! It seems to me that it is only after you have worked your way through interruptions that the day may come when you can hear the voice of an angel sing.

4

Fear

The intriguing part of dealing with an idea honestly is that we don't know where it may take us. There's nothing in manipulating an idea and making it say what we want to hear. Although a scientist goes into a laboratory with certain expectations and hopes, he always keeps open the possibility of a surprise, that perhaps he or she will find something far beyond what she or he ever expected. The same possibility exists when one reads the Bible, lives life, meets people, gets to know oneself.

But most of us like to play it safe; we don't like to take the risks. We want a good job, we want our security taken care of, we want our families to prosper and our children to do well. All of these desires are fine. We would be foolish if we didn't have these goals. But to achieve these goals we try to live in a controlled society. When we do that, we eradicate faith and eliminate the one ingredient that makes life exciting. When we try to control life, it is no wonder that, at times, we can have so many things going for us and feel like nothing matters. Life can be utterly bland. Although we may have more to be thankful for than we have ever had before, the lilt in the living is gone.

We are called to live by faith. Most of us, however, don't really believe that we are. We say, "I know in whom I believe. I know I am saved in this life and the next." We can live according to those statements if we want to, but it will not have much meaning for us or anybody else. We can witness to a lot of other people and they may follow us, but we will have no zest in living.

Jesus lived by faith; there was always risk in his life. "Come, and follow me," he said. Someone asked, "Where do you live?" "Foxes have holes and birds have nests," he replied, "but I don't know where I am going to spend the night." That's risky, isn't it? That's also the adventure, the allure, the invitation; that's Christianity!

There is something inspiring about the Hebrew people's struggle to get out of Egypt, and their years in the wilderness, during which they tried to figure out what they were to do and what God was like. We can call their thinking primitive if we wish, but that group of people was growing, their minds were alive. Regrettably, however, if we are not careful, what happened to them is what happens to all of us when we think we have arrived—we stop living by faith. The Hebrew people went into the land of Canaan, and it became their land of milk and honey; they thought they had arrived. They built a temple and put God in it. Then they stopped looking and stopped living by faith. In effect, they were saying, "We know where God is. Come to our altar. We can tell you what to do. You will find what you need here."

Centuries went by, and Jesus was born. His ability to think was one of the most significant things about him. He was the genius of all life. He was a person who saw life in such utter reality that it made sense to do those things that were ethical, compassionate, and loving. Jesus lived by faith, and he called people to live by faith. He saw a world that has never yet existed. He saw possibilities in people that we have never yet experienced. He saw ideas that we may never fathom, although they might occasionally flit through our minds; he lived by faith.

"Blessed are the meek," he told us. We can respond to that by saying, "Why, if we were meek, the world would kill us; we'd be destroyed!" Perhaps that is true. But suppose we follow that idea, that grain of a mustard seed, the leaven to leaven the bread. Think what the world will have! Following that idea is faith.

Rather than follow Jesus in faith, most of us have done a desperate thing—we have made our religion one of comfort. We think, "Now, I'm secure because I have Jesus. I can get to God through Jesus." But we've toned Jesus down. Jesus didn't ever say that he himself was secure; he spoke of the process of loving. He never said, "Everything will be fine, follow me." Instead he admitted that he did not know where he was going to spend the night. Jesus once asked, "Simon Peter, do you love me?" Simon Peter replied, "Lord, I love you." "Then," Jesus said, "feed my sheep." Where do you find security in that? We know that we are to love people, but we can respond, "Lord, what if people don't love me back?" Jesus might say, "They may not." Where is the security that we want? The security is found in the process of caring, and that is faith.

Jesus faced the cross when he was about thirty-three years old. He knew what was going to happen. He had seen people crucified. He didn't know what was going to happen merely because it had been worked out in the mind of God; the crucifixion was not foreordained. We know that certain things are going to happen in our own lives. Although we are not fortunetellers, we know that certain events are going to occur. For example, a good teacher almost knows the grade that each student will make. There will be some surprises, but the teacher knows the students. Jesus knew the people, he knew his own ideas, and he knew that the people probably weren't going to change. But he was more concerned about showing God to be a God of love and following that in his own life, than going to the cross. That was his top priority, rather than saving his own skin. His sweat was like great drops of blood. He said, "Now, Father, is my soul troubled." That's fear, isn't it?

How do we respond to the idea of our Savior's being scared half to death? Some people can't accept it. To me, that is their problem. The Gospels show that Jesus was frightened. And, if we think that through, we are able to see something of the manhood of the Master. One of the reasons we can love him as we do and call him Savior is that he took a risk. He may have thought, "It might not work, no one may ever follow these teachings, but it doesn't have to work because it is right. Should I say, 'Father, save me from this hour?' No. This is really what I came to do. O God, give me the strength to do it." That is living at its best. But we have been taught that we are not to be afraid.

Let us suppose that a man manipulated his income tax in his own favor. We can imagine that this might happen.

We want to do it legally, of course, and not get into trouble. However, there are certain lines that we might shade periodically. Suppose a man made an adjustment in his own favor, aware of what he has done. But then suppose he becomes fearful, afraid someone may check his tax return and he might get into trouble. And then suppose apprehension takes over and he becomes anxious about this.

A friend of his could see him and wonder why he was nervous, what was worrying him. He doesn't have to tell his friend his problem. He isn't sick or neurotic; he just has a fear for a very real reason. He has done something and he hopes he can get by with it. He is not terrified, but he is afraid. All of us sometimes find ourselves in that situation; for example, when we wait for a doctor's report. We are not going to lose our minds, although we are anxious; we wait and wonder what the report will be. It is normal to be afraid. We shouldn't think that we wouldn't experience fear if we were greater Christians. It is normal, at times, to experience fear and anxiety.

I am not referring to a neurotic fear that can grip us and make us afraid of everything. That is unhealthy. The normal fears that all of us experience are healthy—we need them. Not only that, I think fear is one of the ways that we learn to love, because the more you care about someone, the more you are involved in a risk, and the greater the risk, the more fear you have. Sometimes, the more fear we have, the more faith we may develop.

Let us suppose that someone very dear to you is critically ill. You really don't know whether the person is going to recover, but you care more about that person than you care about yourself. You would be glad to exchange places without any hesitation. You care, you love, and now you are afraid.

Someone could say to you, "Just have faith and get rid of your fear." That can't work because the way you get rid of your fear and your risk is by learning to love less. You are not worried about a lot of people who are sick because you don't care enough about them, not because you have too much fear. We cannot love everyone in the world to the same degree. We have to be that way in order to protect our own lives. The more you care, quite probably, the more fear you will have. But, it is out of that fear and risk that we might develop faith.

Often the reason you are afraid is because you care. If you love, you may recognize that you are frightened. The more you care, the more you are likely to be afraid, because your care and your love may make you vulnerable so that fear can move in.

If we really cared to have world peace, we would be afraid that we might never have it. If we really cared about the mental health of people, we would be concerned that not very many others seem to be concerned. If we really cared about the problems of the handicapped, we wouldn't just walk around our cities and occasionally think about making improvements that could make it easier for them. We have a fear and we hurt if we really care, and out of that hurt, we might develop a faith.

Because of Jesus' concern for his disciples, I think he felt a certain apprehension; he loved so much. He might have said, "Now, Father, what should I say, 'Save me from this hour?' No, not really." He sweated drops of blood. "For this cause came I into the world that You may be known." The next time you are frightened and

someone says, "Have faith!" step back and realize the
reason that you are afraid. It is not because you lack
faith, it might be because you love so deeply. And the
more deeply you love, the more you will be afraid, and
the more you are afraid, believe it or not, the greater
your capacity to have faith.

However, all of us like to minimize our risks, we like
to be safe. That is both understandable and healthy. My
friend Dr. Gaston Foote, was once invited to Texas
Christian University to offer a prayer at the Frog Club,
the booster club for TCU football team. Unfortunately,
the football team had not had a very good year. Dr.
Foote told me that he was originally scheduled to give
the prayer after the TCU–Arkansas game, but he
thought that Arkansas would probably trounce TCU.
Understandably, he didn't want to pray after that game,
so he suggested that he offer a prayer after the upcoming
TCU-Rice game because he thought TCU had a better
chance of beating Rice. Dr. Foote knew when to pray!
To a degree, we are all very much like this.

In addition to wanting to play it safe, we are also
superstitious. We have been led to believe that we can
make something happen by thinking it. If we have an
X-ray taken, someone can say, "Now, you should be
positive about this. Don't let yourself think of negative
results." We're kidding ourselves. The X-ray has already
been taken. Our thoughts have absolutely nothing to do
with whether or not it is going to be a good report.

Of course, there are certain negative things we can
think that can hurt us. If we think we are going to fail in
an endeavor, the chances are good that we will. But we
are incapable of thinking something into existence. We
cannot think a medical report into being good or bad.

We could probably think that someone doesn't like us and, to a degree, make that person not like us. But you cannot think good thoughts about someone and force him or her to love you. While we do not control the world by our thoughts, our thoughts can affect our relationships, and our thoughts do affect our attitude.

A friend of mine once got on an elevator that had stopped at one of the upper floors of a tall building. As the elevator started its descent, he looked around and discovered that there was only one other person on the elevator with him—and that person was rather tough looking. Suddenly, the man demanded that my friend turn over his wallet. He said, "Give me your wallet!" My friend said, "I will not give you my wallet! You give me your wallet!" The man just stood there, presumably because he hadn't expected this kind of response. When the elevator reached the main floor, the man stepped out of the elevator and ran out of the building. That was the end of it.

Obviously, things don't always happen like this. But there are times when your attitude and response can affect a situation and make it better for you. However, we must remember that we do not think everything into existence.

Sometimes events occur over which you have absolutely no control. You apply for a job and you are positive that you are going to get it. But perhaps the man doing the hiring already has someone else in mind for the job and he is just going through the motions of an interview to satisfy other members of the staff. You could have been as positive as you wanted to be about getting this position, but you were never really in the running.

Regrettably, we are so superstitious at times that we frighten ourselves. We are unable to admit our fear, and that makes us neurotic. Many of us are afraid of all kinds of things. We are afraid of the past. Perhaps we did something several years ago and we are afraid somebody will find out about it. Or we are afraid of the present.

There is a story about a man who was being sued. He was given permission to leave town during the litigation, and he asked his attorney to send him word of the outcome as soon as it was known. So, while he was out of town, he received a telegram from his attorney reading "Justice prevails!" In reply he telegraphed, "Appeal immediately!" Each of us reacts that way at times. Even when things go well for us, we try to hide the past, we are frightened in the present, or we are fearful of the future.

I understand that about the only fear a baby has is the fear of falling or of being dropped. As we grow older, one of our main fears is the fear of dying. Although all of us fear dying periodically, I think we are probably more afraid that the people we love may die than we are of our own death. We are afraid of the future, of another war, of inflation, of the energy crisis—we wonder what in the world we will do if things get worse. And then someone may tell us that being Christian means that we are to have faith and not have fear. But, quite honestly, if we had no fear, that would only diminish our capacity to care.

There are a lot of things we are not afraid of, and that is sometimes because we don't care about them—they just don't matter to us. If we care nothing about an ethnic minority group and we hear that their rate of unemployment is increasing, we don't feel apprehension or anxiety. That knowledge does not affect us one way or another because we do not care. The enemy of faith is not fear, it is lack of love, the absence of caring.

I hope we don't ever forget that Jesus knew what it was to be afraid. The reason he could be afraid was that he out-loved all the rest of us. He cared about the world with every ounce of energy. Yet he knew what could happen because of the way people are. And in facing the future, he could sweat, as it were, drops of blood.

Acknowledging the fact that Jesus knew fear should enable us to recognize that our world is a risky world, whether we like it or not. We cannot possibly control everything, although we might like to. If we could control everything, if we covered every base and every possible contingency, our lives would lose their spark.

For example, there are groups of people who are so afraid that the world is coming to an end that they are trying to control everything. In that effort, they build walls around their homes and store up food. Now suppose the nuclear-powered nations do bomb us all to bits and those people are the only ones left. They have armed themselves with guns so that, if any others do survive, they can't come and get any of their food. If you were a survivor, how would you like to visit that group? What kind of an existence are they going to have? What kind of a future population would that remnant of people produce?

No, we cannot be secure in everything. We cannot ever be intelligent enough, or wealthy enough, or have enough answers to every situation so that we are completely protected. Life is always risky.

My mother lives in a small town in Arkansas. There are several women there who are about her age who get together whenever a storm cloud appears. This happens quite frequently, and when any one of the women notices a threatening cloud, she will call the others and they will meet in a storm cellar equipped with a telephone. According to my mother, they get over to the cellar about once a week.

Mother told me that, one time, just as they arrived, one woman turned to her and said, "Marguerite, I'm going to call my home." Mother asked her why and she said she just wanted to make sure that everything was all right.

"But you live by yourself," my mother said. "Surely, you don't expect anybody to be there."

"I'm frightened," the woman replied, "I'm afraid I have a burglar."

"Do you think, in the name of common sense, that a burglar would answer the phone?"

The woman said she didn't know, but she just had to call. So, she picked up the telephone—and dialed a wrong number. When a man answered, the woman asked, "Where are you?"

"I'm at home," the man replied.

"You are lying!" she told him. "You are at my house and you know you are!"

Life is risky, and there is no way that we can get around it. Once in a while, the very things we do to make ourselves feel better scare us half to death. Each one of us is going to be afraid, and we should admit it. But we should take comfort in the fact that we are in great company. I'm not referring to a neurotic fear; quite obviously, our fear should be related to reality.

Another reaction to fear is to want God to control everything because we want security. But God does not work that way. When we are children, we are inclined to think that our parents know everything and can solve every problem. That is probably a good feeling. As we grow older, however, we come to realize that our parents cannot control everything. This realization is disillusioning to teenagers. It is one of the reasons that some of them hate their parents and perhaps never get over this animosity. It seems to them that their parents have deceived them, lied to them. In actuality, their parents were not deceitful, they simply lived as parents. Someone who has known that fear as a child, as a young person, or at any age, must have a God who is in control. Such a person can think, "If my parents can't run everything, I want a big God who can." Now, we can make our God like that if we want to, but that is not an accurate conception of God. God does not work that way. A God who will control everything is not the message of the Bible; it is not the message of Jesus of Nazareth.

We can mentally create whatever "reality" we wish, but to live effectively we have to check our mental image against reality. For instance, we should ask, How did Jesus live? Did God control everything during Jesus' life? To be honest, we would have to say no, he did not. Jesus took risks; he lived for what ought to be, whether it ever developed or not. He said, "Will you come and follow me? I see a world that hasn't been born yet. I see a relationship between people that isn't now in existence. I see you in reality in a way that you have never envisioned." That kind of living is a risk, that's faith; and that is also fear.

Suppose we reach out to love someone, and our

overtures fail—our love is not returned. Rather than risk failure again, we may choose the alternative of playing it safe, or beating everyone. But look at history. How great did Rome look when it conquered other nations? Find an individual who can gobble up all of his competition and see what happens to him, what kind of a person he becomes. Jesus washed his disciples' feet. By contrast, "The greatest among you," he told his disciples, "will be the servant." It is in service that God is found, not in power. God is presence. The most significant thing in the world is love, not muscle. I'm being very practical when I say this, because if we want to live together in our world, it is time we learned to do it as humane people. As long as we are unwilling to face fear, unwilling to risk trying in faith to establish good will, we will never find it.

We can live as previous generations have done, and pass our world on to the next generation. That can go on for hundreds of years. But, eventually, some children will be born who will not think as we do; who, for whatever reason, are not polluted by our thoughts. They will care so much that they will run a risk. Because of this they may get hurt, but though they may be afraid, they will march to the sound of a different drummer.

No, God is not in charge of everything. Instead, God is in everything, trying to get us to be with him through faith and build a greater world. Unfortunately, we cop out. We so often live as selfishly as we want to, and then we ask God to solve our problems.

We are called to live by faith and that is exactly what we ought to do. Living by faith is the most fun, the most exciting thing in the world. It is like a teacher's working with a handicapped child over a long period of time. The teacher doesn't know whether or not the child will be able to learn. The parents don't ask about the child's progress because the efforts at rehabilitation have gone on for so long. Finally, one day the teacher is able to reach the child and the child begins to make some improvement.

Faith is like a woman loving a man when she doesn't know whether or not he will return her love. Living by faith is Jesus calling his disciples to be with him, but giving them the freedom to leave him. It's longing for world peace when we have no assurance that we will attain it. It's wanting to have a friend, but feeling that you might remain alone.

We can play it safe if we want to, but that is not the Christian message. Fear is not the opposite of faith; the opposite of faith is the refusal to care. We are going to run a risk if we care enough. We are going to be afraid if we run a risk. But we should stay in that situation, because out of that fear and risk, we develop a larger capacity to have faith.

"Come and follow me," is Christ's command. We can say, "Lord, before I commit myself, I want to know where you live. What has living the way you do done for you?" Jesus might say, "Come and see." We go part of the way, we look and we really don't see anything. Jesus could say, "That's what I wanted you to see—nothing. Foxes have holes, that's pretty secure; birds have nests, that's also pretty secure. But I don't even know where I am going to spend the night. Now, will you come and follow me?"

That request is full of risk and it frightens us. But, if we care enough and if we love enough, we are going to do as Jesus asks. And, under God, we move out in faith while we are frightened. Maybe God can take that faith and begin to help us build a better society, a better world, and we will become healthier. Don't let people deceive you any longer. The opposite of a great faith is not fear, it is the refusal to love.

5

How Does Jesus Save Us From Our Sins?

In order to think about how Jesus saves us from our sins, let's go back and look at the story of the garden of Eden. We read in Genesis that the garden was perfect. Adam and Eve were in control; they could do whatever they wanted, with one exception—they were told not to eat the fruit of a certain tree. But they did. And then they sensed the presence of God, and became afraid. That is very much like the feeling we have when we feel guilty.

Adam said that Eve made him eat the fruit; that she caused the problem. Eve said she had not caused the problem—the snake did it. Then, according to the story, God said to them: "Since you have wanted to think, since you are trying to become real, I'm going to curse you. Adam will have to work forever. The woman will bear children, her pain will be almost unbearable. And the snake will crawl on his belly forever."

Instead of reaching out, Adam and Eve could have

been docile and sweet and lived in the garden for an indefinite period of time. After all, didn't they have everything they needed? Adam had the whole garden to just have a good time in. His companion, Eve, was so lovely. There were just the two of them to enjoy everything.

However, I thought that it was healthy when a person grew up in a family and then tried to leave home in order to go out on her or his own and do something. I thought there was a sense of adventure in reaching out. Isn't that how we grow? America would not be in existence unless some people had reached out. The trouble with the Prodigal Son is not that he left home, the trouble is with the way he wasted his life after he left home. When a baby is born, we congratulate the parents. Is that birth a curse?

I think we have read the Bible incorrectly and misinterpreted the Fall. Try to read this story from a different point of view. We find the words, "God made everything that was made." Isn't it possible that Adam became frightened in the process of growing? And then God said, "What are you doing, Adam?" Instead of honestly answering, "God, I ate the apple, I thought that thought; I reached out in trying to become," Adam lied. I believe the deception, the lying, is the Fall, rather than the reaching out.

The curse, the Fall is not due to our trying to become. Your eye wants to go to the light; your mind wants to ask questions. A baby is born and he tends to cry because his lungs want to expand. That is not a curse, that is birth. We have treated the desire to move beyond where we are as a curse. We have misread the Book of Genesis and misinterpreted God's message.

Adam and Eve left the garden, and according to the story, they could not return. That is always the way it is. Did you ever try to go back? You cannot. We can think about the good times of the past, the way things used to be, but we cannot actually return to them. Adam and Eve could not go back to where they were and live in their former naïve way. Their minds were questing and, thank God, minds always will.

We once took our family back to the Caddo River in Arkansas. I learned to swim in that river when I was a little boy. I could remember how hard I had struggled to swim from one side of it to the other. It was a sizable river in my mind. I could hardly wait to see that rushing river again, years later, when we took our children back to see it. I think it's quite possible that rivers shrink, because when we arrived at the Caddo River, our son said, "Dad, is that where you learned to swim?" "Barry," I said, "be quiet and get back into the car!"

That is the way life is. Adam and Eve wanted to get back into the garden, but a flaming sword blocked their way. We cannot go back.

We have developed some erroneous ideas by misreading this story. One of those false notions is that we are born with a curse. Some people believe that we are dirty and sinful because we came into the world through sex, and that we must be washed and baptized so that God can take us back. Those people believe that there is a certain amount of naughtiness about our presence. After all, look how we got here! Baptism can almost be conveyed as the idea of bathing us spiritually so that we will be acceptable to God. But a baby really hasn't left God; God is in that child. Reread the Book of

Genesis. The first chapter tells us that God made everything that was made and everything God made was good. We can jump over these words and develop the idea that we are cursed, we are born into sin, we are bad, and we have to flee from the wrath to come. We couldn't be more wrong!

Perhaps one of the reasons that John Wesley never grew very large was that he exhausted himself fleeing from the wrath to come. While he made great contributions to religion in the world, he would have driven most of us crazy if we had lived with him. He was almost like someone with a phobia who felt compelled to constantly wash his hands in an effort to get rid of the dreadful germs. John Wesley repented constantly, trying to escape the wrath to come.

God is not wrathful; we don't have to be afraid that an angry God is going to destroy us. A theology that advocates the theory of an angry God can be found, and statements that support that idea can be read in the Bible, but we should read some other biblical statements along with these, to be accurate. And when we read them, we should get our priorities right.

We find honesty full-grown when we read what Jesus said about himself and his mission: "I have come as light so you don't have to live in darkness any longer." Can't we understand what he is saying? He means, in effect, "I want you to see what I am teaching, but I really want you to see the one who sent me—God. . . . Should you not do what I ask you to do, I will not judge you." Think of that last statement. If God is like Jesus, look again at what Jesus said: "I will not judge you because I did not come to be a judge, I came to be a savior." That means that God is a saving God.

Regrettably, we are often introduced to the basic ideas of life in an erroneous way, and some of us never outgrow that initial false introduction. No wonder that we are sometimes sick and neurotic in our religious approach. And then some of us double our speed because we are lost; we read the Bible more because we have misunderstood it. If we begin with the wrong premise, it won't make any difference if we memorize every word in the Bible.

We have also developed another impression that I think is very destructive—the idea that we will prosper when we are good and we will be hurt when we are bad. One of the problems with this notion is that, if we believe it, then we are not concerned about being good or bad, we simply like the rewards. If we are intelligent, we will realize that this idea doesn't make sense. Some of the best people in the world suffer and some of the worst people prosper. We could ask the age-old question—why is right on the scaffold and wrong on the throne?

Let's look at the flaws in this premise another way. Imagine a high-school girl who, for whatever reason, doesn't have many friends. She is not a member of any club, she is not an outstanding scholar, but she is so very good, kind, and loving. If she sees someone else doing extremely well, she may decide that she is not very good. She may think that if she were a better person, she, too, would be doing well. Some of us have thought this way ourselves. The young girl could then decide that, not only is she not capable, but she must not be good; because, if she were better, God would do more for her. There may be more love in that young girl's heart than in all of our hearts put together, but we do not prosper just because we are good.

Although there were times that he had a temporary kind of success, Jesus did not prosper. Jesus asked one of the most poignant questions mankind has ever heard. One day he turned to his disciples and said, "Are you going to leave me, too?" He was implying, "I can understand why the crowds would abandon me. In a sense, I didn't expect them to stay, particularly when they began to understand what I was saying. But I handpicked each of you—are you going to leave me, too?"

We are supposed to be followers of Jesus. Despite what anyone may say, Jesus was not successful from a worldly point of view. Those who claim that he was are misreading the Bible. He was truth, he was mercy, he was compassion, he was wisdom; he was all of these things of quality, but he was not successful.

If we believe that we will get ahead if we are good enough, we will be frustrated because we will not know how to handle it when we do not prosper. The church never should have supported that idea in the first place. The idea is not, "Come to Christ so that you can get what you want," it is, "Come to Christ so that you can live, so that you can be."

We may fall in love with God through Christ, and it may be a marvelous experience for us. But we may have more problems after that than we have ever had before in our lives. The world is not moved forward because you and I do or do not have problems. Do you think the world is helped by the fact that you receive a salary increase or that I get a promotion? Not at all. Our relationships with people are what makes a difference in the world. The way we look at God, the way we look at others, and the way we look at ourselves makes a difference.

We must dismiss the senseless idea that we will prosper if we are good and suffer if we are bad. Naturally, there are sins we can commit that will hurt us desperately. We are intelligent enough to be aware of that, but that has nothing to do with this false belief. And surely we can realize that there are times when people get ahead magnificently when they have broken almost every rule in the book. That is simply the way life is.

We are frustrated by the threat of another war, inflation, and the energy problem. These things, along with the personal problems that all of us have, frighten us. I was visiting with a friend some time ago. She told me that she had gone to pick up a good friend of hers to go out somewhere together. When she arrived, the lady wasn't quite ready, so my friend went into the house to wait. She said the woman she was picking up was the most meticulous housekeeper imaginable. My friend sat down in the den, saw some fresh fruit, reached over and took an apple and ate it. When she finished the apple, she didn't know where to put the apple core. She went into the kitchen and found a wastebasket inside a cupboard. The wastebasket, lined with pink tissue paper, was empty. She decided that was just too immaculate, she couldn't put the apple core in there. She finally put the apple core in her purse. At times we have a problem that we can't get rid of. Our lives are filled with situations like that.

Sometime ago, Pope John Paul II said that lust was

destructive. While this may be true, we should not consider ourselves sinners because we have strong feelings. We are not sinners because we feel, because we desire, and because we love. Not that at all. A young boy and girl who love each other need to discipline themselves, but feelings of love and sexual desire are not evil. We have labored under the idea of avoiding "that terrible flesh" for so long.

The Pope also supposedly said that a man should not lust after his wife. I will not comment on that statement at length. However, I imagine there are wives who, once in a while, wish their husbands would lust after them. I'm not trying to be facetious, I'm simply trying to make it clear that we are human beings. I don't totally agree with the Pope's statements. I think perhaps we shouldn't make too many rules if we are not going to play the game. We are alive and living in the world, we should not labor under false guilt.

The church can "rev us up" and make us feel guilty for just being. The church says we are not supposed to be homosexual and we are not supposed to be too heterosexual. That doesn't leave us too many choices, does it? We cannot be robots, just walking around being "spiritual" and dying as quickly as possible so that everyone can say we were such lovely human beings. Hitler, as far as we know, did not have very much of a sex drive. He expressed himself in some other ways, didn't he? If we become sick sexually, our anger and hostility will be destructive, we will be vindictive. There is absolutely no reason for us to feel guilty for being.

I am not advocating permissiveness. There are sexual sins that we can commit that would destroy us. But we should know ourselves and allow ourselves to be. We should recognize our anger when we become angry. When we have certain sexual desires, we shouldn't constantly repent because we think we are lustful and God is going to send us to hell. Those very desires can help us to love people and God's world when they are handled properly. The greatest contribution we will ever make to life is when we love. Unfortunately, we are taught that we have to flee from the flesh in order to be spiritual. The truth is that we need to become spiritual in the flesh. Yet so many of us labor under false guilt and want someone to come and save us from this guilt.

One of the ways that Jesus saves us is by letting us see how we are. He shows us that God made us and we are good. For years, the four-minute mile stood as a track record. Finally, one day, a man broke that record. A short time later, three people broke it in another race. I don't think that runners suddenly became that much faster, they just saw that it could be done. That is the way that Jesus lived and taught. He acted love out, rather than just talking about it. The love that he expressed was authentic. He shows us that we are not bad people, we are good.

Although we are good people, there will be times when we ought to get angry, times when we are going to be unhappy, times when we will be depressed or frustrated. We will desire some things we shouldn't; we will be greedy. We don't have to give in to all of these things, but we should recognize them. And when we recognize them, we should not think of ourselves as worms in the dust. We are not born into sin, we are born with potential. I think Jesus breaks the spell of thinking we are bad people if we let him. We get converted by seeing ourselves in a different light.

Not only does Jesus save us by letting us see that we are good people, he also introduces us to a different and better picture of God. We remember that Jesus was in the upper room with his disciples. Normally, if they had had the money, a servant would have been provided to wash their feet. The disciples didn't want to wash each other's feet because they were afraid they would appear degraded. Jesus took a basin and towel and washed their feet. That was the way he judged them.

If people don't do what we want them to do, we might fire them or embarrass them. Look what Jesus did. He didn't wash his disciples' feet to ridicule them—rather, that is how he judges. He said very clearly: "If you don't do what I ask you to do, I don't judge you. I didn't come to judge, I came to be a savior."

A good teacher works in much the same way that Jesus worked. If a child can't solve a problem, he may wait until the other pupils leave the classroom and then go to the teacher's desk. He might tell the teacher that he was having trouble. A good teacher would say, "we'll work on this together," and show the student how to solve the problem. That is learning; that is growth. In the realm of religion, it is salvation; it is the way God works with us. God is a saving God.

We are also saved by Jesus, I think, because he shows us the relationship that we have with God. He shows us that we belong to God.

Quite some time ago, I was sitting at a café counter when a man I knew came in and sat beside me. He looked at me and remarked, "I'm really relieved!" I asked him why and he said that a certain man had come back to work that day. The man had worked for him for thirty years and he had come back that day. I asked him why that was unusual. He said that he had fired the man on Friday because of a disagreement. He was so relieved that the man came back because, he said, "I don't think I could run my business without him." I asked him what he would have done if the man had not come back today. "By noon, I would have gone out and brought him back," he replied.

Now, that employee was fired on Friday. He never discussed his dismissal with his employer, but he came back to work on Monday because he knew he was needed and wanted. Those two men had some kind of relationship! One angry action could not sever their relationship. That is security, and that is very much like our relationship with God. We belong to God. Neither one action nor a series of actions is going to break our relationship with God because he will never let us go. If we make a hell out of our world and our lives, that is our doing and not God's. We want to think and God wants us to think. We fall when we lie and deceive and want to pass the blame somewhere else, not when we grow and know too much.

We can afford to be honest because we have a relationship with God. We are not standing before an enemy. Remember that the way Jesus judged shows us how we are judged. Jesus said, "If you don't do what I ask you to do, I am not going to judge you, because I do not come as a judge. When you see me, you are also seeing the One who sent me." This means that if Jesus is not judging us but helping us, and Jesus is like God, God is a saving God. Think that through.

I believe we are introduced to the God who always has been, but we did not know him. One of the reasons that the world needs Jesus is that no one else ever taught this idea. How does Jesus save us from our sins? By helping us to know that we belong to a God who is a saving God.

6

Coping

Each one of us has had to cope in order to exist. You would not be reading this book today if you had not coped at one time or another. At times we cope because we are almost imprisoned between two emotions—we are threatened by what we know and are anxious about what we do not know. For his followers in this kind of situation, Jesus told the parable of the crafty steward (Luke 16).

The story concerns a man caught in a crisis—he was facing the loss of his job. Apparently he had not handled his responsibilities the way he was supposed to, so his employer called him in and said, "I'm going to relieve you of your job; you're through!" The steward began to think: "What am I going to do? I don't want to dig ditches." He probably hadn't done any physical labor for a long time. Most of us can understand his aversion to being "reduced" to earning a living by physical labor. I could be very much like he was. I could say, "Lord, use me any way you want to," but really mean that I want to be used in an advisory capacity. We're all like that to some degree. We talk about what a marvelous contribution physical labor makes to our lives and the fact that we couldn't get along without it—which is correct—but we don't relish doing it ourselves.

If the steward did lose his job and could not—or would not—do physical labor, begging was the other alternative. But he was too proud to beg. He wondered what other options were open to him. And then he had an idea. He would be clever. He decided he would go to the people who owed his employer money and discount what they owed. So he went to one person and asked, "What do you owe?" The person replied, "One hundred measures of oil." "Write fifty," the steward said. Another debtor owed one hundred measures of wheat, and the steward said, "Write eighty."

After he had done this, the steward went to his employer, told him what he had done, and gave him the money he had collected. The steward was clever because he had assessed his employer pretty accurately. He knew that his employer had cut corners a number of times, and it was clear that he was going to be fired. He decided that he would be nice to the people who owed money to his employer, so that they would be kind to him if he were out of work. That's why he discounted their debts to his employer.

There is a subtle implication in this story. The steward's employer had probably practiced usury, which was a serious offense, to the Jewish mind. Evidently, he tried to legalize his usury by dealing in goods rather than money. Usury was the charging of interest on loans of money. But if you dealt in goods such as wheat or oil, you could bend the law. This was done quite often, and

Jesus came into conflict with the practice periodically. The employer in this story had increased his price not by charging more in dollars and cents, as we would, but in commodities—a hundred barrels of oil, a hundred bushels of wheat.

What the steward did was to cut the charges back to the amount the people actually owed. In other words, he discounted the usurious interest, the cream that his employer would have received. The employer knew that he had overcharged. In essence, the steward was saying to him: "This is what they actually owed you and this is what I have brought to you. What are you going to do about it? If you fire me, they will probably be nice to me and realize that you were trying to take advantage of them. But, if you keep me, you can act pious. They may even think that this was your idea. What are you going to do?" The result was that the employer congratulated the steward.

The lesson in this story is not an easy one to deal with. We know that Jesus is always concerned about morals, about servants, about the meek. He stressed that the most important thing in our lives is how we treat other people; yet in this story he is complimenting a rogue. This story I believe, was not told to create faith, nor is it the kind of story after which you would say, "Go and do likewise." Instead, I think this story was told in order to give encouragement to the faithful when they do not measure up.

Let's be brutally honest with ourselves for a moment and admit that we do not always measure up. We can be born again as many times as we wish, but still our actions do not always measure up to perfection. We cut corners; we take advantage of other people. We are not what we ought to be. Perhaps we are better than some; however, if we have a modicum of self-awareness, we realize that we are not what we ought to be, nor are we what we pretend to be when we talk about how religious we are.

I think Jesus told this parable to say to religious people: "Here is a word of encouragement for those who have tried, done the best they could, and are taking care of themselves when faced with a dilemma. Perhaps you are embarrassed about what you have done. You realize that you were not what you should have been, but you did about as well as you could do. I want you to know that it's going to be all right."

Many of us, however, rather than hear the word of encouragement, try to cope by making religion somber. We labor under the false belief that God is going to treat us better if we are more serious. Instead, we need to realize that we can hardly survive in our day and time without having some degree of flexibility.

Let's look at some of the things we worry about and how we try to cope with them.

How can we begin to handle the financial crunch today? All of us, I suspect, worry about that from time to time. We also worry about our own health or the health of those we love. Sometimes we are anxious about very personal things that we cannot even discuss. Regardless of what it is that distresses us, none of us goes for very long without being under pressure. We know what it is to be in a crisis, to be confronted with a dilemma—and that is the story of this parable. The steward is going to lose his job. He does not want to work physically, and he is too proud to beg. What would your choice be?

Sometimes we joke when we are trying to find some way of coping. That can be both good and bad. It can be good because some humor can be a release for us when we are facing a serious situation. We would have a real problem if we had to live in a crisis situation for a prolonged period of time and had absolutely no sense of humor. However, humor is not good for us if we use it as a defense mechanism to keep other people away—if we joke so that others cannot get close to us.

Suppose that I am facing a tough problem and you are aware of it. You come to me because there is something really vital that you want to tell me and I need to hear it. But, just as you are about to convey this information to me in a way that might come through to me, I crack a joke or kid, and by doing so, keep you from getting close to me. All of us have done that.

Along that line, one of the most normal things that we do periodically is pretend that we are not hurt when we are. We laugh so that we won't cry. Sometimes we grin and walk away from someone or leave a room as quickly as possible because we don't want anyone to see how deeply we are hurt. A sense of humor can be helpful, if it is not carried to an extreme so that we alienate ourselves from others or continually put up a false front.

On the other hand, if you are in a crisis situation and have allowed yourself no humor, you are too tightly strung. It is possible to be too uptight. Granted, our problems may be enormous, but we shouldn't be so very serious, so restricted all the time. We should give ourselves the freedom to joke about our problems once in a while.

Some time ago, the author Gore Vidal announced that he was considering running for the Senate from the State of California. At the same time, he stated that he had not voted since 1964, and that he encouraged other people not to vote. His statement told us a great deal. Quite obviously, most people who intend to run for office do not tell the constituency that they have not voted for a number of years. It did not appear that he was going to get very far in his race, if and when he ran, but his comments were refreshing. By contrast, we can take ourselves far too seriously.

Another way we try to cope is by being in complete control. We do this because we think everything is all right if we are in charge, and also because, the truth is, we like to boss. We like change if we bring it about, but we resist change instigated by others. That is one of the reasons that many children do not like to have their rooms rearranged by anyone. They may want to rearrange their rooms, but they like to keep their rooms and their possessions pretty much as they are. Basically, we like to be in charge, we like to call the shots.

A friend of mine once told me that she had received a very unusual telephone call. Someone called and asked for someone she had never heard of. She told the caller that he had the wrong number. The phone rang again, it was the same person and, once again, she told him he had the wrong number. The phone rang for the third time and, with a slight edge in her voice, she said, "I am sorry, you really do have the wrong number!" "No, I don't," the caller replied, "you picked up wrong." I think I may have met that person; perhaps you have, too. All of us probably know someone who has never made a mistake, who always has to be in control of the situation.

Although we may try to cope by being in charge, it won't work. It may help us temporarily, but we can't always direct everything. We cannot make every decision for our families, our children, our business, or our organization, nor should we. Who has that much authority? Who would really want it? There is a happy medium here; we should be in control part of the time. Just as we shouldn't carry humor to the extreme, we shouldn't carry this to the extreme and allow ourselves to be doormats. In a healthy balance there will be times when we are in control and times when others are calling the shots.

There are also times when we try to cope by being very successful. If we have enough money, we can almost surround ourselves with people who will tell us what we want to hear. However, we are rather protected if we choose this method. We are insulated because, not only will those around us tell us only what we want to hear, but they can also select what we see or are exposed to. This method doesn't work well for very long.

As an example, consider the family of the Shah of Iran. Reportedly they are one of the wealthiest families in the world, yet they must live in fear. They must move periodically from place to place. Obviously, they have the resources to hire an ample number of bodyguards. However, I suppose if someone wants to kill you, he can find an opportunity. With all of their wealth, this family is afraid.

How much wealth would it take to make you feel secure? If you are going to cope by that method, you are not ever going to have enough money. Naturally, we are foolish if we do not recognize the usefulness of having a certain amount of money. The man in the parable was about to lose his source of income. Was he going to beg? You and I don't want to beg either, so we need a certain amount of money in order to live. But we can never amass enough material wealth to cope with everything.

There are some of us who try to cope with a problem by acting tough. I have tried this, and I would imagine that many of you have, too. When we get hurt, we adopt the attitude of a stoic. We just flex our mental muscles and refuse to let anyone hurt us. At best, this only works temporarily.

Trying toughness as a method of coping is observable on the national level. Our country seems to alternate between taking a tough stance with other countries and using a softer approach. Perhaps, at times, we do need to be very tough—I don't know. But if we think for one moment that we can be so tough on our enemies that we can make them do what we want them to do, we had better go back and read history. Quite obviously, if we did away with our armed forces, another country would destroy us immediately. We do need a certain amount of protection. But toughness by itself has never worked very long.

Think about it. You don't like it when someone takes a tough stance with you. You don't like it at all if someone bosses you around, lords it over you, and kicks you around. None of us likes that. Let us suppose you are working for a man who insults you and embarrasses you; he makes you feel degraded. If you have a family to support or don't know where else to go, you may put up with that for a while. You can say, "Yes, sir . . . No, sir . . . Thank you, sir," for just so long; then the day will come when you would almost rather starve than be dehumanized in that way any longer.

While we do need firmness, toughness by itself will not suffice. Try it with your friends, your parents, or your business associates, and see what you achieve. Yet, as with every other way of coping, we do need a balance. We are not wise unless we realize that there are times when we need to be firm. There are times when we need to hold fast and say to someone, "I'm not going to let you hurt me any longer; this is it, I'm drawing the line."

Many of us try to be religious in order to cope. That can work for us, to a degree, as long as we also use our minds. Unfortunately, many of us try to adopt a mindless religion. We can say, as we have heard others say: "I have given my whole life to God and now he is thinking for me." God is not thinking for you. If we think, "God, I've turned everything over to you, now you are responsible for me," who are we kidding? If we go out and drive our cars, how well do you think God will drive?

If God is going to be working through us, we would have to assume that we have a perfect understanding of God, which none of us can claim. God may want to communicate with us, but none of us has perfect knowledge, or perfect hearing ability, or perfect powers of assimilation. We should use our minds. We should become religious, but we should become religious with some sense. We should not become religious and surrender the use of our minds; we should not give up the ability to think and to reason.

And, very much like the steward in the parable, we sometimes try to cope by being clever. We, too, can come up with schemes to try to protect ourselves or insure our futures. All of us employ various methods in our attempts to cope.

It is clear from our varying approaches to ways of coping that there is no single solution. However, I would like to make several suggestions. First of all, I think it is important that we live a day at a time. Obviously, you got through yesterday, and you are probably going to get through tomorrow. So let tomorrow take care of itself; live today.

We would crumble if we took the past and the future and brought them together. No one could stand that. How could anyone exist if he dug back into the past and remembered all the pains and sadness that he had gone through? If we brought that to the surface of our minds and then added the apprehensions of the future, we wouldn't be able to cope with anything that happened today. A healthy person is someone who can recall the past, have some goals for the future, and live in the present with a certain amount of flexibility.

I recently took a course studying the artist Marcel Duchamp. During one class period, the professor flashed a picture of one of Duchamp's paintings on the wall. The artist had painted on glass, and I thought I saw broken pieces of glass in the painting. There were many cracks in it that appeared real to me. Later, I found out that they *were* real.

Duchamp had worked on this particular painting for quite some time. One day, when it was being transported from one art gallery to another, the truck carrying it was involved in a collision and the painting was broken—hence all the cracks. When the artist saw what had happened to the painting he had so arduously created, he didn't have a nervous breakdown. He said, "Ah, that completes my painting!" It was hung in an art museum just as it was.

That is a pretty neat way to live. Duchamp gave himself that day. And we can give ourselves today in the same way. That advice is scriptural. The prophets in the

Old Testament talked about it. Jesus talked about it. How do you cope? You can live in God's world *today*.

Another suggestion is to remind ourselves that whatever we are experiencing right now, regardless of what it might be, will not last forever. If we are happy right now, that reminder could make us sad. But if we are sad or depressed right now, there is hope, because we won't have to live like this forever. Your joy may pass away, but it will come again. We are not going to experience the same emotion every day of our lives. In that sense, nothing is permanent. In the midst of depression, remembering that it will not last is a good way to cope.

I would also like to suggest that we be good to ourselves—simply that. Unfortunately, the church has stressed for too long what you and I owe to the world. It is obvious that we owe love, compassion, and concern to all people. Yet Jesus, the master at living, told the parable of the steward. It's here and we mustn't water it down.

In a sense the story Jesus told is out of character for him. Jesus was concerned about morals and ethics. In fact, he was more concerned about them than anyone I have ever known or heard of. He wants us to be good people because being good people helps us to be healthy people. But he didn't impose restrictions upon us. Instead, he lifted guilt. He tried to give us a better understanding of ourselves, a better picture of ourselves. That's why I'm suggesting being good to yourselves as a way of coping. We need to remember that when bad things happen to us, we are not causing all of them, and the gods are not against us, nor is God against us. When two or three unfortunate things happen to us in a row, it is easy to think that our luck is bad and always will be. That is not true. Be good to yourself and remember that. At times, someone may not like you and may try to hurt you, but he or she is not in charge of your life. Remind yourself of that. Be good to yourself.

When Jesus told this story, I think he intended it for those of us who want to be the right kind of person and who have tried hard to be that kind of person. Perhaps we have cut a few corners, not always been truthful, not always been fair, and taken advantage of other people. Jesus is telling us that we have shortchanged ourselves, too, and we are not aware of it. We have been hard on ourselves. This story is for the religious person, it offers encouragement to the faithful. We should be good to ourselves, nice to ourselves.

We have not always measured up and been the kind of people that we ought to be; we know that and God knows that. But we shouldn't try to give reasons for what we have done. There are no excuses; we just did it. And then one day we turn to God. God is the employer of the story, and that's why Jesus told it. And, surprisingly, we are congratulated, not because we were clever or because we were able to cope, but because of who we are.

We should be as moral as we can be and as ethical as we can be; we should continually work on ourselves. Let justice, compassion, and love burn like a fire in our lives. We should be concerned about issues, have high ideals and never lower them. Yet when we, as individuals, don't measure up, we can still go trustfully to God. I believe that for many reasons—one of which is that Jesus told this story. When we admit what we have done,

I think we will be shocked, just as the steward was shocked when his employer congratulated him after he had told him what he had done.

When we go to God, he will not congratulate us for making mistakes, but he will welcome us back home. You can hardly ask for a better way of coping than that.